Slow Cooker Cookbook for beginners UK

600-Day Easy, Mouth Watering and Healthy Recipes to Cook Entrees, Sauces, Soup, Meat, Vegetables, and More.

Evans Deony

Table of Contents

INTRODUCTION

With today's fast-paced society, it's a struggle for anyone to slow down.

There are just too many things to do, and it seems like time is never enough to accomplish everything.

But it does pay off to take things slow from time to time, like with home cooking.

Slow cooking, which is a cooking method that allows you to make flavorful dishes without the hassle, can actually be a timesaver. This is because even with the long duration of cooking, the active preparation usually required for each meal is minimal.

Most of the work is done by the slow cooker.

Not to mention, you also get to enjoy nutritious and affordable meals that are good for your health, as well as for your budget.

In this book, you'll learn the basics of cooking with the slow cooker, and you'll find out for yourself why it's good to slow down whenever you have the chance.

Enjoy slow cooking!

Chapter 1: An Overview of the Slow Cooker

Also known as the crockpot, the slow cooker was first introduced in the 1970s. But it's only been in the recent decade that it has become popular again. And it's not a surprise why.

As most people lack the time and energy to cook elaborate dishes at home, the slow cooker has become a viable solution. This cooking device can help anyone prepare flavor-packed dishes without too much trouble, something that busy people are thankful for.

Plus, it helps families save money too. This cooking method works well with cheap meat cuts, and at the same time, consumes less energy than an electric oven.

What is a Slow Cooker?

A slow cooker is an electric cooking appliance that is used to simmer food at low temperature for long duration. The slow and low method of cooking allows for the tenderizing of the meat and ingredients, which is also why this is used for making beef stews, pot roasts and other similar dishes.

Of course, this is not the only thing that slow cookers can do. A slow cooker can also be used to make delicious soups, dips, casseroles, and even bread.

And because it cooks food for long hours, you're free to do other things at home like clean the house, do any chores, or attend to work you've taken home. All these you can do while the food is simmering away in the slow cooker.

It's also a good thing that slow cooker manufacturers have made the device even easier for beginners to use than when it was first introduced in the market decades ago. Set up and operating the device is simple even for those who have never tried slow cooking before.

Buying a Slow Cooker

There are many factors that you have to consider when buying a slow cooker.

One of the most important considerations is the size. If you are cooking for one or two people, you can invest in a small slow cooker—3 quart or 4 quart. But if you're cooking for a family such as for four to five people, then it would be a good idea to buy a 5 quart or 6 quart slow cooker.

Quality is also another factor you can't overlook. A slow cooker is a cooking device that should be made using the highest standards of quality and safety so that you don't put your family at risk while you're using it inside your home. Invest in brands that are reputable, and are known to have good reviews. It pays to take the time to read online reviews about different slow cooker brands so you can make an informed buying decision.

It would also be a smart move to look for features such as removable cord, cool to touch handles, and dishwasher safe removable inserts so that using the device would be easy as well as convenient for you.

Care and Maintenance Guidelines

The modern-day slow cooker is much easier to clean and maintain than the first models that came out many years ago.

Here are some cleaning and care tips that you should keep in mind:

- Clean after using. Let the slow cooker cool for a few minutes. Once cool enough to handle, remove the lid and crock. Wash these with warm water and soap. Using a damp cloth, wipe the outside of the cooking element.

- For tough stains, clean with a mixture of baking soda and water. Use a soft bristle brush to carefully remove the food debris.

- If there are too many tough spots, you can soak the pot with water mixed with a little vinegar and baking soda. Let it soak for one hour. After this, you can wipe off the debris.

- To save time, you can also make of slow cooker liners. This makes cleanup a lot more convenient.

Benefits of Using Slow Cooker

There are many benefits to using a slow cooker. Here are some of them that would convince you why this cooking appliance should definitely be part of your kitchen.

- Encourages your family to eat at home. Sometimes, you get too caught up with so many things to do at work and at home that you barely have time to do any cooking. Even during weekends, it seems like there's not enough time accomplish everything that you and your family end up eating in restaurants most of the time. But if you have a slow cooker at home, cooking can be a breeze. You simply have to prepare the ingredients in advance, dump them all in the slow cooker and let it do the rest of the work. Before you know it, you're enjoying flavorful dish that everyone will enjoy.

- Provides health benefits. As long as you use healthy ingredients and lean meat and you tone down on salt and sugar for flavoring, your slow cooker can become your ally when it comes to shifting towards a healthier diet. And because you're eating at home more often, you get to enjoy nutritious homemade meals.

- Infuses dishes with flavor. Slow cooking brings out natural flavors of meat and other ingredients. Simmering the ingredients together for long hours

combines flavors.

- Ensures convenient cleanup. Not only do you get to save time with food preparation, you also don't have to exert much effort with the cleanup. You will only be using one pot to cook the entire meal.

- Allows for batch cooking. With a slow cooker, you can cook a big batch of meal that you can freeze to serve for the next few days. This means you only have to cook one night a week, and the rest of the days, you simply have to reheat food. This is a great solution for those with overloaded schedule.

- Saves money. As mentioned earlier, slow cookers use less electricity than electric ovens. This means lower electricity bills for the household. Not only that, with the slow cooker, you can cook tough meat cuts which are typically cheaper than other cuts. Examples are roasts and chuck steaks. These are easily tenderized through the slow cooking method.

As you can see there are many advantages to using a slow cooker, which is why, you don't have to think twice about investing in this cooking appliance, and making it part of your kitchen arsenal.

Chapter 2: Cooking Tips and Guidelines

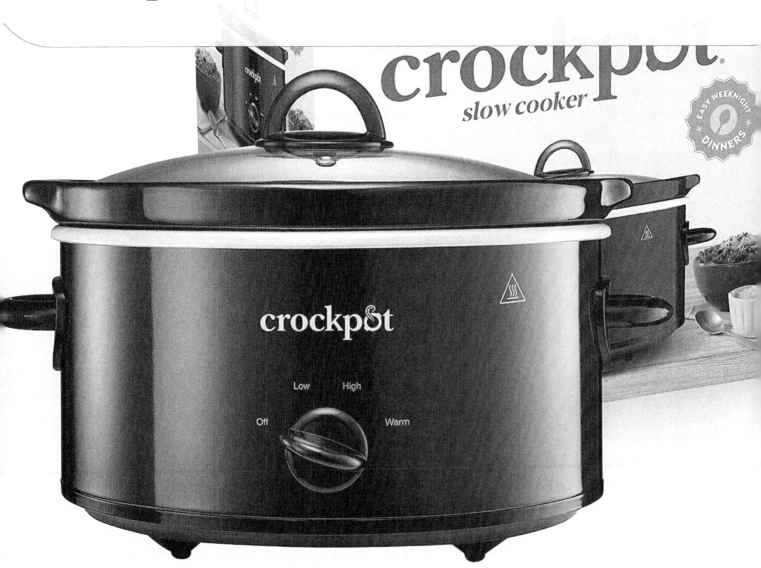

Cooking with a slow cooker is not rocket science. You don't have to be a kitchen pro to achieve cooking success with this incredible device. Most of the slow cookers that you'll find in the market today are very easy to operate, and come with safety features that did not exist when the slow cooker first came out in the market.

To help you with your cooking, here are some tips and guidelines to follow. Heed these tips to be able to cook with the slow cooker with ease and convenience.

How to Cook with a Slow Cooker

Here are the steps on how to cook using the slow cooker:

1.Prepare the ingredients

Slice the ingredients uniformly. This helps to ensure even cooking. Thaw the meat, chicken or frozen vegetables that you will use before cooking these in the slow cooker. It takes too long for slow cooker to cook frozen food.

2.Fill the slow cooker

Fill the pot at least half full or up to three quarters full. Use ½ cup to 1 cup less liquid than what you usually use for other cooking methods. Keep in mind that because the air circulating inside the pot creates steam, this adds more liquid to the dish.

3.Operate the slow cooker

Follow the manual or recipe when it comes to setting the temperature and time for the dish. Make sure that you follow these steps. You don't want to risk your family's health with undercooked dishes.

Tips for Cooking Success

- Place the lid on top of the slow cooker when cooking. Not only does this ensure that the heat stays inside, and that the proper cooking temperature is maintained, this also keeps unwanted elements outside your dish.

- Avoid opening the slow cooker while cooking unless specified in the recipe that you are using. Every time you peek into the dish, heat would escape and you will need to cook for an additional of 30 minutes. You'd want to check the dish for doneness in the last hour or minutes of cooking instead.

- Do not over fill your slow cooker. Just like with any other cooking appliance, it's never a good idea to over fill your slow cooker. See to it that you don't fill it more than ¾ full. When you overfill the slow cooker, food won't cook evenly. Also, the fewer the ingredients are inside the pot, the faster cooking will be done.

- Place the tough meat cuts and hard vegetables like carrots, potatoes or sweet potatoes at the bottom of the slow cooker. This way, these ingredients will be closer to heat. Softer ingredients like leafy greens should be on top, or can be added later on. Be sure to follow the recipe instructions when it comes to the order of ingredient placement.

Low or High Cook Settings

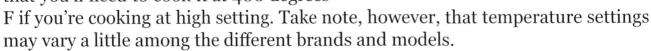

Most recipes that require cooking in the slow cooker takes twice longer to cook on low setting than in the high setting. For example, if you're asked to cook on low setting at 200 degrees F, it means that you'll need to cook it at 400 degrees F if you're cooking at high setting. Take note, however, that temperature settings may vary a little among the different brands and models.

For most dishes, using the low setting results in a dish that's not only more flavorful, but also has better texture. Choosing between the two settings depends on a number of things, including your schedule. If you're on a rush, then you'd want to cook using high setting. But if you have all day to stay at home, then go ahead and use the low setting.

Slow Cooker Food & Cooking Safety Tips

• Food safety

As we all know, we can't just let a dish sit out there for hours as this will cause bacteria to dangerously spread. But how about when you use a slow cooker to cook a dish for long hours?

Keep in mind that bacteria spread when food is 40 degrees F to 140 degrees F. This is why, slow cookers are designed to maintain temperature between 165 degrees F and 200 degrees F. With this temperature, bacteria won't be able to survive.

Aside from food safety, here are some frequently asked questions about the safety of slow cooking.

• Is it safe to leave a slow cooker cooking or turned on overnight?

Slow cookers have been designed for countertop cooking for long duration. When cooking using a stove or an oven, you want to keep a close eye on what you're cooking.

But it's not the same case with the slow cooker. You can leave a slow cooker for long hours. Not to mention, most slow cookers in the market have automatic shut off feature that turns off the device after 24 hours of cooking so there's not much to worry about.

• Is it safe to leave the house with the slow cooker cooking?

If you intend to go outside for more than an hour, see to it that you set your slow cooker to low and that you place it on top of a heatproof surface, and away from walls, or any flammable material. But of course, to be safe, it would be best not to leave the house when using the slow cooker.

● Is it safe to use old slow cooker?

It's no longer recommended to use vintage slow cookers from the 1970s. Even if you think that it's still in good condition and you can see that the cord is not frayed and the appliance is still intact, you'll still be better off with a new slow cooker. Old models do not have the safety features that the new models have. It's always better to be safe than sorry.

● Is it safe to use the slow cooker for cooking frozen food?

There would be times when you'll be tempted to directly place frozen meat or vegetables inside the slow cooker. Resist the temptation. According to cooking experts, it's safer to thaw meat or vegetables first before cooking in the slow cooker. This is because it takes a long time for the slow cooker to cook frozen foods to reach a safe temperature.

● Can you use the slow cooker without adding any liquid?

It's always a must to add liquid in the slow cooker. This will make sure that the ingredients will not get too hot and will not stick to the bottom of the pot. You don't want your dish to burn. You can use water, sauce or broth. Using broth not only infuses the ingredients with flavor, but will also tenderize meat. Opt for low-sodium broth so you can make your dish healthier.

● How much food can I put inside the slow cooker?

As mentioned earlier, you should never fill the pot more than three-fourths full. And this is not only because of even cooking, but also because of safety reasons. When you overfill the pot, this can lead to spills and

messes, as well as undercooked food that might put your family at risk of food-borne illness.

- **Can I cook a whole chicken using the slow cooker?**

It's safe to use large pieces of meat or chicken in the slow cooker. However, it would be safer and more practical to slice the meat into smaller pieces. It's also more convenient. You might find it hard to fit a whole chicken inside the pot.

- **Should I keep the lid on while cooking?**

Uncovering the slow cooker while it's cooking lets the heat escape and in turn, slows down the cooking process. It's best that you keep the lid on throughout the duration of the cooking. Test for doneness in the last hour, or in the last few minutes of cooking.

Preparing Meals Ahead

Yes, you can make slow cooker meals ahead of time! In fact, you can do most of the prep work the night before. For example, you can already prepare the sauce, slice the meat or chop the vegetables.

Just make sure that when you prepare the ingredients, you store them properly. Seal them in a food container or put them in a bowl and cover with foil or plastic, and then place inside the refrigerator.

See to it though that you don't place the ingredients in the slow cooker insert before refrigerating. If you cook with a cold insert, it would take the slow cooker a longer time to heat up. Plus, it's also possible for the insert to crack due to sudden temperature changes.

Getting the Best Flavor

Slow cooking gives you meals that are loaded with flavors. But how you can achieve this also takes a few tricks. Here are some of them:

- Brown the meat before adding to the slow cooker. This technique intensifies the flavor. Aside from that, it also lessens oiliness of the dish.

- Sauté vegetables before using. It would also be a good idea to sauté first the vegetables in olive oil or butter before adding to the pot. But just make sure that the vegetables are still crispy.

- Trim excess fat. You don't want your dish to be too fatty or oily. It would help to remove and get rid of meat fat. You can also let food rest for up to 10 minutes so you can skim off the fat on the top surface.

- Do not overcook meat. You want meat to be tender but not overly dried. It would help to use a meat thermometer. For example, chicken is done once it reaches 165 degrees F. If you cook it longer, it dries up and becomes bland.

- Drizzle with lemon juice and season with fresh herbs. These are a great way to add flavors to slow cooked dishes.

Chapter 3: Breakfast

Breakfast Quinoa Pudding

Prep Time: 10 Minutes
Cook Time: 1 Hour And 30 Minutes
Serves: 2

Ingredients:

- 1/4 cup maple syrup
- 3 cups almond milk
- 1 cup quinoa
- 2 tablespoons vanilla extract

Directions:

1. Put quinoa in your slow cooker.
2. Add maple syrup and almond milk and stir.
3. Also add vanilla extract, stir, cover and cook on High for 1 hour and 30 minutes.
4. Stir your pudding again, divide into bowls and serve.

Enjoy!

Nutritional Value (Amount per Serving):

Calories: 140; Fat: 2g; Carb: 5g; Protein: 5g

Lentils Sandwich

Prep Time: 10 Minutes
Cook Time: 1 Hour And 30 Minutes
Serves: 4

Ingredients:

- For the sauce:
- 1/2 cup blackstrap molasses
- 28 ounces canned tomatoes, crushed
- 6 ounces tomato paste
- 1/4 cup white vinegar
- 2 tablespoons apple cider vinegar
- 1 sweet onion, chopped
- 3 garlic cloves, minced
- 1 teaspoon dry mustard
- 1 tablespoon coconut sugar
- 1/4 teaspoon red pepper flakes
- A pinch of sea salt
- 1/4 teaspoon liquid smoke
- A pinch of cayenne
- 4 cups green lentils, cooked and drained

Directions:

1. Put molasses in your slow cooker.
2. Add tomatoes, tomato paste, vinegar, apple cider vinegar, onion, garlic, mustard, sugar, salt, pepper flakes, cayenne and liquid smoke.
3. Stir everything, cover your slow cooker and cook on High for 1 hour and 30 minutes.
4. Add lentils, stir gently, divide on vegan buns and serve for breakfast.
Enjoy!

Nutritional Value (Amount per Serving):

Calories: 150; Fat: 3g; Carb: 6g; Protein: 7g

Incredible Rice Pudding

Prep Time: 10 Minutes
Cook Time: 3Hours
Serves: 2

Ingredients:

- 1/2 cup coconut sugar
- 2 cups almond milk
- 1/2 cup brown rice
- 1 teaspoon vanilla extract
- 1 tablespoons flax seed meal
- 1/2 cup raisins
- 1 teaspoon cinnamon powder

Directions:

1. Put the milk in your slow cooker.
2. Add rice and sugar and stir well.
3. Also, add flaxseed meal, raisins, vanilla and cinnamon, stir, cover and cook on Low for 2 hours.
4. Stir your pudding again, cover and cook on Low for 1 more hour.
5. Divide into bowls and serve.
Enjoy!

Nutritional Value (Amount per Serving):

Calories: 160; Fat: 2g; Carb: 8g; Protein: 12g

Cornbread Casserole

Prep Time: 10 Minutes
Cook Time: 2 Hours And 30 Minutes
Serves: 6

Ingredients:

- 3 garlic cloves, minced
- 1 green bell pepper, chopped
- 1 yellow onion, chopped
- 15 ounces canned black beans, drained
- 15 ounces canned red kidney beans, drained
- 15 ounces canned pinto beans, drained
- 15 ounces canned tomatoes, chopped
- 10 ounces tomato sauce
- 10 ounces canned corn, drained
- 2 teaspoons chili powder
- 1 teaspoon hot sauce
- A pinch of salt and pepper
- 1/2 cup yellow corn meal
- 1/2 cup almond flour
- 1 and 1/4 teaspoons baking powder
- 1 tablespoon palm sugar
- 3/4 cup almond milk
- 1 tablespoon chia seeds
- 1 and 1/2 tablespoons vegetable oil
- Cooking spray

Directions:

1. Heat up a pan over medium high heat, add garlic, bell pepper and onions, brown them for 7 minutes and transfer them to your slow cooker after you've sprayed with cooking spray.
2. Add black beans, pinto beans, red kidney beans, tomatoes, tomato sauce,

corn, chili powder, salt, pepper and hot sauce, stir, cover and cook on High for 1 hour.

3. Meanwhile, in a bowl, mix almond flour with cornmeal, baking powder, sugar, milk, chia seeds and vegetable oil and stir really well.

4. Add this to the slow cooker and spread.

5. Cover slow cooker again and cook on High for 1 hour and 30 minutes more.

6. Leave your cornbread to cool down before slicing and serving.

Enjoy!

Nutritional Value (Amount per Serving):

Calories: 240; Fat: 4g; Carb: 6g; Protein: 9g

Banana and Coconut Oatmeal

Prep Time: 10 Minutes
Cook Time: 7 Hours
Serves: 6

Ingredients:

- 2 cups bananas, peeled and sliced
- 28 ounces canned coconut milk
- 1 cup steel cut oats
- 1/2 cup water
- 2 tablespoons palm sugar
- 1 and 1/2 tablespoons coconut butter
- 1/4 teaspoon nutmeg, ground
- 1/2 teaspoon cinnamon powder
- 1 tablespoon flax seed, ground
- 1/2 teaspoon vanilla extract
- A pinch of sea salt
- Chopped walnuts for serving
- Cooking spray

Directions:

1. Grease your slow cooker with cooking spray and add coconut milk.
2. Also, add bananas, oats, water, palm sugar, coconut butter, cinnamon, nutmeg, flax seed and a pinch of salt. Stir, cover and cook on Low for 7 hours. Divide into bowls and serve with chopped walnuts on top.

Enjoy!

Nutritional Value (Amount per Serving):

Calories: 150; Fat: 2g; Carb: 5g; Protein: 7g

Blueberry Butter

Prep Time: 10 Minutes
Cook Time: 6 Hours
Serves: 12

Ingredients:

- 5 cups blueberries puree
- 2 teaspoons cinnamon powder
- Zest from 1 lemon
- 1 cup coconut sugar
- 1/2 teaspoon nutmeg, ground
- 1/4 teaspoon ginger, ground

Directions:

1. Put blueberries in your slow cooker, cover and cook on Low for 1 hour.
2. Stir your berries puree, cover and cook on Low for 4 hours more.
3. Add sugar, ginger, nutmeg and lemon zest, stir and cook on High uncovered for 1 hour more.
4. Divide into jars, cover them and keep in a cold place until you serve it for breakfast.

Enjoy!

Nutritional Value (Amount per Serving):

Calories: 143; Fat: 2g; Carb: 3g; Protein: 4g

Carrot Oatmeal

Prep Time: 10 Minutes
Cook Time: 7 Hours
Serves: 3

Ingredients:

- 2 cups coconut milk
- 1/2 cup old fashioned rolled oats
- 1 cup carrots, chopped
- 2 tablespoons agave nectar
- 1 teaspoon cardamom, ground
- A pinch of saffron
- Some chopped pistachios
- Cooking spray

Directions:

1. Spray your slow cooker with some cooking spray and add coconut milk.
2. Also, add oats, carrots, agave nectar, cardamom and saffron.
3. Stir, cover and cook on Low for 7 hours.
4. Stir oatmeal again, divide into bowls and serve with chopped pistachios on top.

Enjoy!

Nutritional Value (Amount per Serving):

Calories: 140; Fat: 2g; Carb: 4g; Protein: 5g

Breakfast Quinoa

Prep Time: 10 Minutes
Cook Time: 8 Hours
Serves: 4

Ingredients:

- 2 cups water
- 1 cup coconut milk
- 2 tablespoons maple syrup
- 1 cup quinoa, rinsed
- 1 teaspoon vanilla extract
- Berries for serving

Directions:

1. Put the water in your slow cooker.
2. Add milk, maple syrup and quinoa, stir, cover and cook on Low for 8 hours.
3. Fluff quinoa mix a bit, divide into bowls, add vanilla extract, stir and serve with your favorite berries on top.

Enjoy!

Nutritional Value (Amount per Serving):

Calories: 120; Fat: 2g; Carb: 4g; Protein: 4g

Pumpkin Butter

Prep Time: 10 Minutes
Cook Time: 4 Hours
Serves: 5

Ingredients:

- 2 teaspoons cinnamon powder
- 4 cups pumpkin puree
- 1and 1/4 cup maple syrup
- 1/2 teaspoon nutmeg
- 1 teaspoon vanilla extract

Directions:

1. In your slow cooker, mix pumpkin puree with maple syrup and vanilla extract, stir, cover and cook on High for 4 hours.
2. Add cinnamon and nutmeg, stir, divide into jars and serve for breakfast! Enjoy!

Nutritional Value (Amount per Serving):

Calories: 120; Fat: 2g; Carb: 4g; Protein: 2g

Mexican Breakfast

Prep Time: 10 Minutes
Cook Time: 2 Hours
Serves: 4

Ingredients:

- 1 cup brown rice
- 1 cup onion, chopped
- 2 cups veggie stock
- 1 red bell pepper, chopped
- 1 green bell pepper, chopped
- 4 ounces canned green chilies, chopped
- 15 ounces canned black beans, drained
- A pinch of salt
- Black pepper to the taste
- For the salsa:
- 3 tablespoons lime juice
- 1 avocado, pitted, peeled and cubed
- 1/2 cup cilantro, chopped
- 1/2 cup green onions, chopped
- 1/2 cup tomato, chopped
- 1 poblano pepper, chopped
- 2 tablespoons olive oil
- 1/2 teaspoon cumin

Directions:

1. Put the stock in your slow cooker. Add rice, onions and beans, stir, cover and cook on High for 1 hour and 30 minutes.
2. Add chilies, red and green bell peppers, a pinch of salt and black pepper, stir, cover again and cook on High for 3 o minutes more.
3. Meanwhile, in a bowl, mix avocado with green onions, tomato, poblano

pepper, cilantro, oil, cumin, a pinch of salt, black pepper and lime juice and stir really well.

4. Divide rice mix into bowls; top each with the salsa you have just made and serve.

Enjoy!

Nutritional Value (Amount per Serving):

Calories: 140; Fat: 2g; Carb: 5g; Protein: 5g

Tofu Burrito

Prep Time: 10 Minutes
Cook Time: 8 Hours
Serves: 4

Ingredients:

- 15 ounces canned black beans, drained
- 2 tablespoons onions, chopped
- 7 ounces tofu, drained and crumbled
- 2 tablespoons green bell pepper, chopped
- 1/2 teaspoon turmeric
- 3/4 cup water
- 1/4 teaspoon smoked paprika
- 1/4 teaspoon cumin, ground
- 1/4 teaspoon chili powder
- A pinch of salt and black pepper
- 4 gluten free whole wheat tortillas serving
- Avocado, chopped for serving
- Salsa for serving

Directions:

1. Put black beans in your slow cooker.
2. Add onions, tofu, bell pepper, turmeric, water, paprika, cumin, chili powder, a pinch of salt and pepper, stir, cover and cook on Low for 8 hours.
3. Divide this on each tortilla, add avocado and salsa, wrap, arrange on plates and serve.

Enjoy!

Nutritional Value (Amount per Serving):

Calories: 130; Fat: 4g; Carb: 5g; Protein: 4g

Cherry Oatmeal

Prep Time: 10 Minutes
Cook Time: 8 Hours And 10 Minutes
Serves: 4

Ingredients:

- 2 cups almond milk
- 2 cups water
- 1 cup steel cut oats
- 2 tablespoons cocoa powder
- 1/3 cup cherries, pitted
- 1/4 cup maple syrup
- 1/2teaspoon almond extract
- For the sauce:
- 2 tablespoons water
- 1 and 1/2 cups cherries, pitted and chopped
- 1/4 teaspoon almond extract

Directions:

1. Put the almond milk in your slow cooker.
2. Add 2 cups water, oats, cocoa powder, 1/3 cup cherries, maples syrup and 1/2 teaspoon almond extract.
3. Stir, cover and cook on Low for 8 hours.
4. In a small pan, mix 2 tablespoons water with 1 and 1/2 cups cherries and 1/4 teaspoon almond extract, stir well, bring to a simmer over medium heat and cook for 10 minutes until it thickens.
5. Divide oatmeal into breakfast bowls, top with the cherries sauce and serve.

Enjoy!

Nutritional Value (Amount per Serving):

Calories: 150; Fat: 1g; Carb: 6g; Protein: 5g

Carrot and Zucchini Breakfast

Prep Time: 10 Minutes
Cook Time: 8 Hours
Serves: 4

Ingredients:

- 1 and 1/2 cups almond milk
- 1/2 cup steel cut oats
- A pinch of nutmeg, ground
- 1 small zucchini, grated
- 1 carrot, grated
- A pinch of cloves, ground
- 2 tablespoons agave nectar
- 1/2 teaspoon cinnamon powder
- 1/4 cup pecans, chopped

Directions:

1. Put the milk in your slow cooker and mix with oats, zucchini, carrots, nutmeg, cloves, cinnamon and agave nectar.
2. Stir, cover and cook on Low for 8 hours.
3. Add pecans, stir gently, divide into bowls and serve right away.
Enjoy!

Nutritional Value (Amount per Serving):

Calories: 120; Fat: 1g; Carb: 5g; Protein: 8g

Quinoa and Cranberries Breakfast

Prep Time: 10 Minutes
Cook Time: 4 Hours
Serves: 4

Ingredients:

- 1/4 cup cranberries, dried
- 1/8 cup coconut flakes
- 1/8 cup almonds, sliced
- 3 teaspoons agave nectar
- 1 cup quinoa
- 3 cups water
- 1 teaspoon vanilla extract

Directions:

1. Put the water in your slow cooker.
2. Add quinoa, vanilla extract, cranberries, coconut flakes, agave nectar and almonds, stir, cover and cook on Low for 4 hours.
3. Fluff quinoa with a fork before dividing into bowls and serving.
Enjoy!

Nutritional Value (Amount per Serving):

Calories: 120; Fat: 2g; Carb: 6g; Protein: 7g

Banana Bread

Prep Time: 10 Minutes
Cook Time: 4 Hours
Serves: 6

Ingredients:

- 3 bananas, peeled and mashed
- 1 teaspoon baking powder
- 1/2 teaspoon baking soda
- 2 cups whole wheat flour
- 1 cup palm sugar
- 2 tablespoons flax meal + 1 tablespoon water
- 1/2 cup coconut butter, melted

Directions:

1. In a bowl, mix sugar with flour, baking soda and baking powder and stir.
2. Add flax meal mixed with the water, butter and bananas, stir really well and pour the mix into a greased round pan that fits your slow cooker.
3. Arrange the pan into your slow cooker, cover and cook on Low for 4 hours.
4. Leave your bread to cool down, slice and serve it for breakfast.
Enjoy!

Nutritional Value (Amount per Serving):

Calories: 160; Fat: 3g; Carb: 7g; Protein: 6g

Chapter 4: Side Dish

Collard Greens

Prep Time: 10 Minutes
Cook Time: 4 Hours And 5 Minutes
Serves: 4

Ingredients:

- 1 tablespoons olive oil
- 1 cup yellow onion, chopped
- 16 ounces collard greens
- 2 garlic cloves, minced
- A pinch of sea salt
- Black pepper to the taste
- 14 ounces veggie stock
- 1 bay leaf
- 1 tablespoon agave nectar
- 3 tablespoon balsamic vinegar

Directions:

1. Heat up a pan with the oil over medium high heat, add onion, stir and cook for 3 minutes. Add collard greens, stir, cook for 2 minutes more and transfer to your slow cooker.
2. Add garlic, salt, pepper, stock and bay leaf, stir, cover and cook on Low for 4 hours.
3. In a bowl, mix vinegar with agave nectar and whisk well.
4. Add this to collard greens, stir, divide between plates and serve.
Enjoy!

Nutritional Value (Amount per Serving):

Calories: 130; Fat: 1g; Carb: 5g; Protein: 3g

Mexican Black Beans

Prep Time: 10 Minutes
Cook Time: 10 Hours
Serves: 4

Ingredients:

- 1 pound black beans, soaked overnight and drained
- A pinch of sea salt
- Black pepper to the taste
- 3 cups veggie stock
- 2 cups yellow onion, chopped
- 1 tablespoon canned chipotle chili pepper in adobo sauce
- 4 garlic cloves, minced
- 1 tablespoon lime juice
- 1/2 cup cilantro, chopped
- 1/2 cup pumpkin seeds

Directions:

1. Put the beans in your slow cooker.
2. Add a pinch of salt, black pepper, onion, stock, garlic and chipotle chili in adobo sauce.
3. Stir, cover and cook on Low for 10 hours.
4. Add lime juice and mash beans a bit using a potato masher.
5. Add cilantro, stir gently, divide between plates and serve with pumpkin seeds on top.

Enjoy!

Nutritional Value (Amount per Serving):

Calories: 150; Fat: 3g; Carb: 7g; Protein: 5g

Mashed Potatoes

Prep Time: 10 Minutes
Cook Time: 6 Hours
Serves: 12

Ingredients:

- 3 pounds russet potatoes, peeled and cubed
- 6 garlic cloves, chopped
- 28 ounces veggie stock
- 1 bay leaf
- 1 cup coconut milk
- 1/4 cup coconut butter
- A pinch of sea salt
- White pepper to the taste

Directions:

1. Put potatoes in your slow cooker.
2. Add stock, garlic and bay leaf, stir, cover and cook on Low for 6 hours.
3. Drain potatoes, discard bay leaf, return them to your slow cooker and mash using a potato masher.
4. Meanwhile, put the coconut milk in a pot, stir and heat up over medium heat.
5. Add coconut butter and stir until it dissolves.
6. Add this to your mashed potatoes, season with a pinch of salt and white pepper, stir well, divide between plates and serve as a side dish.

Enjoy!

Nutritional Value (Amount per Serving):

Calories: 1535; Fat: 4g; Carb: 10g; Protein: 4g

Barley and Squash Gratin

Prep Time: 10 Minutes
Cook Time: 7 Hours
Serves: 12

Ingredients:

- 2 pounds butternut squash, peeled and cubed
- 1 yellow onion, cut into medium wedges
- 10 ounces spinach
- 1 cup barley
- 14 ounces veggie stock
- 1/2 cup water
- A pinch of salt
- Black pepper to the taste
- 3 garlic cloves, minced

Directions:

1. Put squash pieces in your slow cooker.
2. Add barley, spinach, stock, water, onion, garlic, salt and pepper, stir, cover and cook on Low for 7 hours.
3. Stir this mix again, divide between plates and serve.
Enjoy!

Nutritional Value (Amount per Serving):

Calories: 200; Fat: 3g; Carb: 13g; Protein: 7g

Beans, Carrots and Spinach Side Dish

Prep Time: 10 Minutes
Cook Time: 4 Hours
Serves: 6

Ingredients:

- 5 carrots, sliced
- 1 and 1/2 cups great northern beans, dried, soaked overnight and drained
- 2 garlic cloves, minced
- 1 yellow onion, chopped
- Salt and black pepper to the taste
- 1/2 teaspoon oregano, dried
- 5 ounces baby spinach
- 4 and 1/2 cups veggie stock
- 2 teaspoons lemon peel, grated
- 3 tablespoons lemon juice
- 1 avocado, pitted, peeled and chopped
- 3/4 cup tofu, firm, pressed, drained and crumbled
- 1/4 cup pistachios, chopped

Directions:

1. In your slow cooker, mix beans with onion, carrots, garlic, salt, pepper, oregano and veggie stock, stir, cover and cook on High for 4 hours.
2. Drain beans mix, return to your slow cooker and reserve 1/4 cup cooking liquid.
3. Add spinach, lemon juice and lemon peel, stir and leave aside for 5 minutes.
4. Transfer beans, carrots and spinach mixture to a bowl, add pistachios, avocado, tofu and reserve cooking liquid, toss, divide between plates and serve as a side dish.

Enjoy!

Nutritional Value (Amount per Serving):

Calories: 319; Fat: 8g; Carb: 43g; Protein: 17g

Scalloped Potatoes

Prep Time: 10 Minutes
Cook Time: 4 Hours
Serves: 8

Ingredients:

- Cooking spray
- 2 pounds gold potatoes, halved and sliced
- 1 yellow onion, cut into medium wedges
- 10 ounces canned vegan potato cream soup
- 8 ounces coconut milk
- 1 cup tofu, crumbled
- 1/2 cup veggie stock
- Salt and black pepper to the taste
- 1 tablespoons parsley, chopped

Directions:

1. Coat your slow cooker with cooking spray and arrange half of the potatoes on the bottom.
2. Layer onion wedges, half of the vegan cream soup, coconut milk, tofu, stock, salt and pepper.
3. Add the rest of the potatoes, onion wedges, cream, coconut milk, tofu and stock, cover and cook on High for 4 hours.
4. Sprinkle parsley on top, divide scalloped potatoes between plates and serve as a side dish.

Enjoy!

Nutritional Value (Amount per Serving):

Calories: 306; Fat: 14g; Carb: 30g; Protein: 12g

Sweet Potatoes Side Dish

Prep Time: 10 Minutes
Cook Time: 3 Hours
Serves: 10

Ingredients:

- 4 pounds sweet potatoes, thinly sliced
- 3 tablespoons stevia
- 1/2 cup orange juice
- A pinch of salt and black pepper
- 1/2 teaspoon thyme, dried
- 1/2 teaspoon sage, dried
- 2 tablespoons olive oil

Directions:

1. Arrange potato slices on the bottom of your slow cooker.
2. In a bowl, mix orange juice with salt, pepper, stevia, thyme, sage and oil and whisk well.
3. Add this over potatoes, cover slow cooker and cook on High for 3 hours.
4. Divide between plates and serve as a side dish.

Enjoy!

Nutritional Value (Amount per Serving):

Calories: 189; Fat: 4g; Carb: 36g; Protein: 4g

Cauliflower And Broccoli Side Dish

Prep Time: 10 Minutes
Cook Time: 3 Hours
Serves: 10

Ingredients:

- 4 cups broccoli florets
- 4 cups cauliflower florets
- 14 ounces tomato paste
- 1 yellow onion, chopped
- 1 teaspoon thyme, dried
- Salt and black pepper to the taste
- 1/2 cup almonds, sliced

Directions:

1. In your slow cooker, mix broccoli with cauliflower, tomato paste, onion, thyme, salt and pepper, toss, cover and cook on High for 3 hours.
2. Add almonds, toss, divide between plates and serve as a side dish.
Enjoy!

Nutritional Value (Amount per Serving):

Calories: 177; Fat: 12g; Carb: 10g; Protein: 7g

Orange Carrots

Prep Time: 10 Minutes
Cook Time: 8 Hours
Serves: 12

Ingredients:

- 3 pounds carrots, peeled and cut into medium pieces
- A pinch of sea salt
- Black pepper to the taste
- 2 tablespoons water 1/2 cup agave nectar
- 2 tablespoons olive oil
- 1/2 teaspoon orange rind, grated

Directions:

1. Put the oil in your slow cooker and add the carrots.
2. In a bowl mix agave nectar with water and whisk well.
3. Add this to your slow cooker as well.
4. Also, add a pinch of sea salt and black pepper, stir gently everything, cover and cook on Low for 8 hours.
5. Sprinkle orange rind all over, stir gently, divide on plates and serve.
Enjoy!

Nutritional Value (Amount per Serving):

Calories: 140; Fat: 2g; Carb: 4g; Protein: 6g

Black Eyed Peas

Prep Time: 10 Minutes
Cook Time: 8 Hours
Serves: 6

Ingredients:

- 3 cups black eyed peas
- A pinch of salt
- Black pepper to the taste
- 2 cups veggie stock
- 2 tablespoons jalapeno peppers, chopped
- 2 cups sweet onion, chopped
- 1/2 teaspoon thyme, dried
- 4 garlic cloves, minced
- 1 bay leaf
- Hot sauce to the taste

Directions:

1. Put the peas in your slow cooker.
2. Add a pinch of salt, black pepper, stock, jalapenos, onion, garlic, thyme and bay leaf.
3. Stir everything, cover and cook on Low for 8 hours.
4. Drizzle hot sauce over peas, stir gently, divide between plates and serve. Enjoy!

Nutritional Value (Amount per Serving):

Calories: 130; Fat: 2g; Carb: 7g; Protein: 7g

Flavored Beets

Prep Time: 10 Minutes
Cook Time: 8 Hours
Serves: 6

Ingredients:

- 6 beets, peeled and cut into wedges
- A pinch of sea salt
- Black pepper to the taste
- 2 tablespoons lemon juice
- 2 tablespoons olive oil
- 2 tablespoons agave nectar
- 1 tablespoon cider vinegar
- 1/2 teaspoon lemon rind, grated
- 2 rosemary sprigs

Directions:

1. Put the beets in your slow cooker.
2. Add a pinch of salt, black pepper, lemon juice, oil, agave nectar, rosemary and vinegar. Stir everything, cover and cook on Low for 8 hours.
3. Add lemon rind, stir, divide between plates and serve.

Enjoy!

Nutritional Value (Amount per Serving):

Calories: 120; Fat: 1g; Carb: 6g; Protein: 6g

Beans and Lentils

Prep Time: 10 Minutes
Cook Time: 7 Hours And 10 Minutes
Serves: 6

Ingredients:

- 2 tablespoons thyme, chopped
- 1 tablespoon olive oil
- 1 cup yellow onion, chopped
- 5 cups water 5 garlic cloves, minced
- 3 tablespoons cider vinegar
- 1/2 cup tomato paste
- 1/2 cup maple syrup
- 3 tablespoons soy sauce
- 2 tablespoons Korean red chili paste
- 2 tablespoons dry mustard
- 1 and 1/2 cups great northern beans
- 1/2 cup red lentils

Directions:

1. Heat up a pan with the oil over medium high heat, add onion, stir and cook for 4 minutes.
2. Add garlic, thyme, vinegar and tomato paste, stir, cook for 5 minutes more and transfer to your slow cooker.
3. Add lentils and beans to your slow cooker and stir.
4. Also add water, maple syrup, mustard, chili paste and soy sauce, stir, cover and cook on High for 7 hours.
5. Stir beans mix again, divide between plates and serve.

Enjoy!

Nutritional Value (Amount per Serving):

Calories: 160; Fat: 2g; Carb: 7g; Protein: 8g

Sweet Potatoes Dish

Prep Time: 10 Minutes
Cook Time: 6 Hours
Serves: 6

Ingredients:

- 4 pounds sweet potatoes, peeled and sliced
- 1/2 cup orange juice
- 3 tablespoons palm sugar
- 1/2 teaspoon thyme, dried
- A pinch of sea salt
- Black pepper to the taste
- 1/2 teaspoon sage, dried
- 2 tablespoons olive oil

Directions:

1. Put the oil in your slow cooker and add sweet potato slices.
2. In a bowl, mix orange juice with palm sugar, thyme, sage, a pinch of salt and black pepper and whisk well.
Add this over potatoes, toss to coat, cover slow cooker and cook on Low for 6 hours.
3. Stir sweet potatoes mix again, divide between plates and serve.
Enjoy!

Nutritional Value (Amount per Serving):

Calories: 160; Fat: 3g; Carb: 6g; Protein: 9g

Wild Rice

Prep Time: 10 Minutes
Cook Time: 6 Hours
Serves: 12

Ingredients:

- 42 ounces veggie stock
- 1 cup carrot, shredded
- 2 and 1/2 cups wild rice
- 4 ounces mushrooms, sliced
- 2 tablespoons olive oil
- 2 teaspoons marjoram, dried
- A pinch of sea salt
- Black pepper to the taste
- 2/3 cup cherries, dried
- 1/2 cup pecans, chopped
- 2/3 cup green onions, chopped

Directions:

1. Put the stock in your slow cooker.
2. Add rice, carrots, mushrooms, oil, salt, pepper marjoram.
3. Stir, cover and cook on Low for 6 hours.
4. Add cherries and green onions, stir, cover slow cooker and leave it aside for 10 minutes.
5. Divide wild rice between plates and serve with chopped pecans on top. Enjoy!

Nutritional Value (Amount per Serving):

Calories: 140; Fat: 2g; Carb: 6g; Protein: 7g

Wild Rice Mix

Prep Time: 10 Minutes
Cook Time: 6 Hours
Serves: 12

Ingredients:

- 40 ounces veggie stock
- 2 and 1/2 cups wild rice
- 1 cup carrot, shredded
- 4 ounces mushrooms, sliced
- 2 tablespoons olive oil
- 2 teaspoons marjoram, dried and crushed
- Salt and black pepper to the taste
- 2/3 cup dried cherries
- 1/2 cup pecans, toasted and chopped
- 2/3 cup green onions, chopped

Directions:

1. In your slow cooker, mix stock with wild rice, carrot, mushrooms, oil, marjoram, salt, pepper, cherries, pecans and green onions, toss, cover and cook on Low for 6 hours.
2. Stir wild rice one more time, divide between plates and serve as a side dish.

Enjoy!

Nutritional Value (Amount per Serving):

Calories: 169; Fat: 5g; Carb: 28g; Protein: 5g

Chapter 5: Soup & Stew

Southwestern Tomato Carrots Soup

Prep Time: 10 Minutes
Cook Time: 6 Hours
Serves: 2

Ingredients:

- 4 oz can tomatoes, deiced
- 1/4 cup carrots, sliced
- 14 oz vegetable broth
- 1/2 tbsp Worcestershire sauce
- 1 garlic clove, minced
- 1/2 cup potatoes, diced
- 1/4 cup onion, diced

Directions:

1. Add tomatoes and remaining ingredients into the slow cooker and stir well.
2. Cover lid on, and cook on low- temperature mode for 6 hours.
3. Serve warm.

Nutritional Value (Amount per Serving):

Calories: 87; Fat: 1.2g; Carb: 13.5g; Protein: 5.5g

Tomato Green Beans Barley Soup with Ham

Prep Time: 10 Minutes
Cook Time: 4 Hours
Serves: 2

Ingredients:

- 7 oz can green beans, chopped
- 1/4 cup ham, chopped
- 1 1/2 cups tomatoes, crushed
- 1/4 cup barley, uncooked
- 12 oz chicken broth
- Pepper
- Salt

Directions:

1. Add beans, ham, tomatoes, barley, broth, pepper, and salt into the slow cooker and stir well.
2. Cover lid on, and cook on low- temperature mode for 4 hours.
3. Serve warm.

Nutritional Value (Amount per Serving):

Calories: 281; Fat: 3g; Carb: 47.2g; Protein: 17.1g

Mexican Vegetable Bean Chicken Soup

Prep Time: 10 Minutes
Cook Time: 4 Hours
Serves: 2

Ingredients:

- 1 chicken breast, cooked and shredded
- 1/2 cup frozen peas
- 1/2 cup frozen corn
- 7 oz can black beans
- 8 oz chunky salsa
- 16 oz vegetable broth
- 1 packet taco seasoning

Directions:

1. Add chicken, salsa, broth, taco seasoning, peas, corn, and black beans into the slow cooker and stir well.
2. Cover lid on, and cook on low- temperature mode for 4 hours.
3. Serve warm.

Nutritional Value (Amount per Serving):

Calories: 288; Fat: 3.9g; Carb: 38.5g; Protein: 26.9g

Fresh Mixed Vegetable Soup

Prep Time: 10 Minutes
Cook Time: 8 Hours
Serves: 2

Ingredients:

- 1 small carrot, diced
- 1/4 cup can tomatoes, diced
- 2 cup vegetable stock
- 1 parsnip, diced
- 1 celery stalk, diced
- 1 tbsp fresh dill
- 1 shallot, minced
- 1 garlic clove, minced
- 1/4 cup celery, cubed
- 1/4 tsp white pepper
- 1 tsp celery flakes
- 1/8 tsp salt

Directions:

1. Add parsnip and other vegetable dices and remaining ingredients into the slow cooker and stir them well.
2. Cover lid on, and cook on low- temperature mode for 8 hours.
3. Serve warm.

Nutritional Value (Amount per Serving):

Calories: 102; Fat: 0.6g; Carb: 23g; Protein: 2.9g

Brown Curried Cauliflower Soup

Prep Time: 10 Minutes

Cook Time: 6 Hours

Serves: 2

Ingredients:

- 1/2 lb cauliflower florets
- 1 1/2 tsp curry powder
- 1 garlic clove, minced
- 1/2 onion, minced
- 1 1/4 cup vegetable stock
- 1/8 tsp cumin powder

Directions:

1. Add cauliflower florets and remaining ingredients into the slow cooker and stir them well.
2. Cover lid on, and cook on low- temperature mode for 6 hours.
3. Put the mixture into a blender until smooth. If the soup is too soup, you may add water.
4. Serve warm.

Nutritional Value (Amount per Serving):

Calories: 51; Fat: 0.5g; Carb: 10.6g; Protein: 3.1g

Flavored and Fresh Lamb Chicken Stew

Prep Time: 10 Minutes

Cook Time: 6 Hours

Serves: 6

Ingredients:

- 3 lbs lamb shoulder, chopped
- 4 cups chicken broth
- 28 oz tomatoes, diced
- 2 onions, diced
- 4 garlic cloves, chopped
- 2 cups white wine
- 1 bay leaf
- 1/2 Tsp thyme, dried
- 1 tsp fresh thyme
- 1 tsp oregano, dried
- Pepper
- Salt

Directions:

1. Add meat pieces and remaining ingredients into the slow cooker and stir them well.
2. Cover lid on, and cook on low- temperature mode for 6 hours.
3. Serve warm.

Nutritional Value (Amount per Serving):

Calories: 556; Fat: 17.9g; Carb: 12.4g; Protein: 68.7g

Creamy Spicy Carrot Soup

Prep Time: 10 Minutes
Cook Time: 3 Hours
Serves: 4

Ingredients:

- 6 carrots, chopped
- 1 cup coconut milk
- 1 tbsp ginger, chopped
- 1 tsp smoked paprika
- 1 garlic clove
- 1/3 cup water
- 1 tsp salt

Directions:

1. Add carrots and remaining ingredients into the slow cooker and stir them well.
2. Cover lid on, and cook on low- temperature mode for 3 hours.
3. Put the mixture into a blender until smooth.
4. Serve warm.e warm.

Nutritional Value (Amount per Serving):

Calories: 183; Fat: 14.5g; Carb: 13.8g; Protein: 2.4g

Green Bean Soup with Tomato and Carrots

Prep Time: 10 Minutes

Cook Time: 6 Hours

Serves: 8

Ingredients:

- 1 lb fresh green beans, cut into 1-inch-sized pieces
- 3 cups fresh tomatoes, diced
- 1 cup carrots, chopped
- 1 cup onions, chopped
- 1/4 tsp black pepper
- 1 tsp basil, dried
- 1 garlic clove, minced
- 6 cups chicken stock soup
- 1/2 tsp salt

Directions:

1. Add green beans, tomatoes and carrots, and remaining ingredients into the slow cooker and stir well.
2. Cover lid on, and cook on low- temperature mode for 6 hours.
3. Serve warm.

Nutritional Value (Amount per Serving):

Calories: 71; Fat: 1.3g; Carb: 10.2g; Protein: 5.6g

Cheese Chicken Soup

Prep Time: 10 Minutes
Cook Time: 4 Hours
Serves: 6

Ingredients:

- 1 1/2 lbs chicken, boneless & cut into pieces
- 15 oz chunky salsa
- 8 oz pepper jack cheese, grated
- 15 oz chicken stock

Directions:

1. Place chicken into the slow cooker.
2. Pour remaining ingredients over the chicken, covering the chicken breasts. Add some water if needed.
3. Cover lid on, and cook on high- temperature mode for 4 hours.
4. Shred the chicken by a fork.
5. Serve warm.

Nutritional Value (Amount per Serving):

Calories: 342; Fat: 15.9g; Carb: 4.7g; Protein: 43.6g

Easily- made Asparagus Soup

Prep Time: 10 Minutes

Cook Time: 4 Hours

Serves: 4

Ingredients:

- 1 lb asparagus, trimmed and chopped
- 2 cups chicken stock soup
- 2 tbsp olive oil
- 1/2 cup onion, chopped
- 1/4 tsp pepper
- 1/2 tsp salt

Directions:

1. Add asparagus and remaining ingredients into the slow cooker and stir them well.
2. Cover lid on and cook on high- temperature mode for 4 hours.
3. Puree the soup by a blender until smooth.
4. Serve warm.

Nutritional Value (Amount per Serving):

Calories: 108; Fat: 7.8g; Carb: 6.3g; Protein: 5.1g

Curried Tomato Soup

Prep Time: 10 Minutes
Cook Time: 4 Hours
Serves: 8

Ingredients:

- 4 lbs tomatoes, diced
- 2 tsp curry powder
- 2 cups coconut milk
- 1 cup water
- 2 tbsp onion, minced
- 1 tsp garlic, minced
- 1 tsp salt

Directions:

1. Add tomatoes and remaining ingredients into the slow cooker and stir them well.
2. Cover lid on, and cook on high- temperature mode for 4 hours.
3. Puree the soup by a blender until smooth and thick.
4. Serve warm.

Nutritional Value (Amount per Serving):

Calories: 182; Fat: 14.8g; Carb: 12.8g; Protein: 3.5g

Asparagus and Cauliflower Soup

Prep Time: 10 Minutes
Cook Time: 6 Hours
Serves: 2

Ingredients:

- 1 lb asparagus, cut into 1/2-inch- sized pieces
- 1 cup cauliflower, chopped
- 3 cups vegetable broth
- 1 large onion, chopped & sauteed
- 2 tbsp olive oil
- 1 lemon juice
- Pepper
- Salt

Directions:

1. Add asparagus and remaining ingredients into the slow cooker and stir well.
2. Cover lid on and cook on low- temperature mode for 6 hours.
3. Puree the soup by a blender until smooth.
4. Add in pepper and salt for better flavor.
5. Serve warm.

Nutritional Value (Amount per Serving):

Calories: 45; Fat: 2.8g; Carb: 3.4g; Protein: 2.4g

Healthy Broccoli Spinach Soup

Prep Time: 10 Minutes
Cook Time: 4 Hours 30 Minutes
Serves: 6

Ingredients:

- 2 1/2 cups broccoli florets
- 5 oz baby spinach
- 1 cup onion, chopped
- 4 1/2 cups vegetable broth
- 3 garlic cloves, minced
- 1/2 tsp pepper
- 1 1/2 tsp salt

Directions:

1. Trim the broccoli, leaving the florets.
2. Add broccoli florets, onion, broth, garlic, pepper, and salt into the slow cooker and stir well.
3. Cover lid on, and cook on high- temperature mode for 4 hours.
4. Add spinach and cook for 30 minutes more.
5. Puree the soup by a blender until smooth.
6. Serve and enjoy.

Nutritional Value (Amount per Serving):

Calories: 58; Fat: 1.3g; Carb: 6.5g; Protein: 5.7g

Chicken Soup with Mixed Vegetable

Prep Time: 10 Minutes
Cook Time: 3 Hours 30 Minutes
Serves: 4

Ingredients:

- 1/2 lb chicken breasts, boneless& skin less& diced
- 8 oz mushrooms, sliced
- 2 carrots, chopped
- 2 celery stalks, chopped
- 2 cups water
- 4 cups chicken stock soup
- 1 onion, chopped
- 4 green onions, diced
- 1/2 tsp pepper
- 1 tsp salt

Directions:

1. Add chicken and remaining ingredients except the vegetables into the slow cooker and stir them well.
2. Cover lid on, and cook on high- temperature mode for 3 hours.
3. Add green onions, mushrooms and carrots and stir well.
4. Cover lid again and cook for 30 minutes more.
5. Serve warm.

Nutritional Value (Amount per Serving):

Calories: 189; Fat: 5.8g; Carb: 9.9g; Protein: 23.9g

Easily- made Sweet Potato Soup

Prep Time: 10 Minutes

Cook Time: 4 Hours

Serves: 4

Ingredients:

- 2 lbs sweet potatoes, peeled and chopped
- 4 cups vegetable broth
- 4 leeks, sliced
- 1 tbsp olive oil
- 1/2 tsp thyme powder
- 1/4 tsp pepper
- 1 1/2 tsp garlic salt

Directions:

1. Add sweet potatoes and remaining ingredients into the slow cooker and stir them well.
2. Cover lid on, and cook on low- temperature mode for 4 hours.
3. Puree the soup by a blender until smooth.
4. Serve warm.

Nutritional Value (Amount per Serving):

Calories: 394; Fat: 5.6g; Carb: 77.7g; Protein: 9.9g

Chapter 6: Snack And Appetizer

Chipotle Tacos

Prep Time: 10 Minutes
Cook Time: 4 Hours
Serves: 4

Ingredients:

- 30 ounces canned pinto beans, drained
- 3/4 cup chili sauce
- 3 ounces chipotle pepper in adobo sauce, chopped
- 1 cup corn
- 6 ounces tomato paste
- 1 tablespoon cocoa powder
- 1/2 teaspoon cinnamon, ground
- 1 teaspoon cumin, ground
- 8 vegan taco shells
- Chopped avocado, for serving

Directions:

1. Put the beans in your slow cooker.
2. Add chili sauce, chipotle pepper, corn, tomato paste, cocoa powder, cinnamon and cumin.
3. Stir, cover and cook on Low for 4 hours. Divide beans and chopped avocado into taco shells and serve them.

Enjoy!

Nutritional Value (Amount per Serving):

Calories: 342; Fat: 3g; Carb: 12g; Protein: 10g

Spinach Dip

Prep Time: 10 Minutes
Cook Time: 4 Hours
Serves: 12

Ingredients:

- 8 ounces baby spinach
- 1 small yellow onion, chopped
- 8 ounces vegan cashew mozzarella, shredded
- 8 ounces tofu, cubed
- 1 cup vegan cashew parmesan cheese, grated
- 1 tablespoon garlic, minced
- A pinch of cayenne pepper
- A pinch of sea salt
- Black pepper to the taste

Directions:

1. Put spinach in your slow cooker. Add onion, cashew mozzarella, tofu, cashew parmesan, salt, pepper, cayenne and garlic.
2. Stir, cover and cook on Low for 2 hours.
3. Stir your dip well, cover and cook on Low for 2 more hours.
4. Divide your spinach dip into bowls and serve.
Enjoy!

Nutritional Value (Amount per Serving):

Calories: 200; Fat: 3g; Carb: 6g; Protein: 8g

Sweet and Spicy Nuts

Prep Time: 10 Minutes
Cook Time: 2 Hours
Serves: 20

Ingredients:

- 1 cup almonds, toasted
- 1 cup cashews
- 1 cup pecans, halved and toasted
- 1 cup hazelnuts, toasted and peeled
- 1/2 cup palm sugar
- 1 teaspoon ginger, grated
- 1/3 cup coconut butter, melted
- 1/2 teaspoon cinnamon powder
- 1/4 teaspoon cloves, ground
- A pinch of salt
- A pinch of cayenne pepper

Directions:

1. Put almonds, pecans, cashews and hazelnuts in your slow cooker.
2. Add palm sugar, coconut butter, ginger, salt, cayenne, cloves and cinnamon.
3. Stir well, cover and cook on Low for 2 hours.
4. Divide into bowls and serve as a snack.
Enjoy!

Nutritional Value (Amount per Serving):

Calories: 110; Fat: 3g; Carb: 5g; Protein: 5g

Corn Dip

Prep Time: 10 Minutes
Cook Time: 2 Hours And 15 Minutes
Serves: 8

Ingredients:

- 2 jalapenos, chopped
- 45 ounces canned corn kernels, drained
- 1/2 cup coconut milk
- 1 and 1/4 cups cashew cheese, shredded
- A pinch of sea salt
- Black pepper to the taste
- 2 tablespoons chives, chopped
- 8 ounces tofu, cubed

Directions:

1. In your slow cooker, mix coconut milk with cashew cheese, corn, jalapenos, tofu, salt and pepper, stir, cover and cook on Low for 2 hours.
2. Stir your corn dip really well, cover slow cooker again and cook on High for 15 minutes.
3. Divide into bowls, sprinkle chives on top and serve as a vegan snack! Enjoy!

Nutritional Value (Amount per Serving):

Calories: 150; Fat: 3g; Carb: 8g; Protein: 10g

Butternut Squash Spread

Prep Time: 10 Minutes
Cook Time: 6 Hours
Serves: 4

Ingredients:

- 1/2 cup butternut squash, peeled and cubed
- 1/2 cup canned white beans, drained
- 1 tablespoon water
- 2 tablespoons coconut milk
- A pinch of rosemary, dried
- A pinch of sage, dried
- A pinch of salt and black pepper

Directions:

1. In your slow cooker, mix beans with squash, water, coconut milk, sage, rosemary, salt and pepper, toss, cover and cook on Low for 6 hours.
2. Blend using an immersion blender, divide into bowls and serve cold as a party spread.

Enjoy!

Nutritional Value (Amount per Serving):

Calories: 182; Fat: 5g; Carb: 12g; Protein: 5g

Cashew And White Bean Spread

Prep Time: 10 Minutes
Cook Time: 7 Hours
Serves: 4

Ingredients:

- 1/2 cup white beans, dried
- 2 tablespoons cashews, soaked for 12 hours and blended
- 1 teaspoon apple cider vinegar
- 1 cup veggie stock
- 1 tablespoon water

Directions:

1. In your slow cooker, mix beans with cashews and stock, stir, cover and cook on Low for 6 hours.
2. Drain, transfer to your food processor, add vinegar and water, pulse well, divide into bowls and serve as a spread.

Enjoy!

Nutritional Value (Amount per Serving):

Calories: 221; Fat: 6g; Carb: 19g; Protein: 3g

Vegan Rolls

Prep Time: 10 Minutes
Cook Time: 8 Hours
Serves: 4

Ingredients:

- 1 cup brown lentils, cooked
- 1 green cabbage head, leaves separated
- 1/2 cup onion, chopped
- 1 cup brown rice, already cooked
- 2 ounces white mushrooms, chopped
- 1/4 cup pine nuts, toasted
- 1/4cup raisins
- 2 garlic cloves, minced
- 2 tablespoons dill, chopped
- 1 tablespoon olive oil
- 25 ounces marinara sauce
- A pinch of salt and black pepper
- 1/4 cup water

Directions:

1. In a bowl, mix lentils with onion, rice, mushrooms, pine nuts, raisins, garlic, dill, salt and pepper and whisk well.
2. Arrange cabbage leaves on a working surface, divide lentils mix and wrap them well.
3. Add marinara sauce and water to your slow cooker and stir.
4. Add cabbage rolls, cover and cook on Low for 8 hours.
5. Arrange cabbage rolls on a platter, drizzle sauce all over and serve.
Enjoy!

Nutritional Value (Amount per Serving):

Calories: 261; Fat: 6g; Carb: 12g; Protein: 3g

Colored Stuffed Bell Peppers

Prep Time: 10 Minutes
Cook Time: 4 Hours
Serves: 5

Ingredients:

- 1 yellow onion, chopped
- 2 teaspoons olive oil
- 2 celery ribs, chopped
- 1 and 1/2 teaspoon oregano, dried
- 2 cups white rice, already cooked
- 1 cup corn
- 1 tomato chopped
- 7 ounces canned pinto beans, drained
- 1 chipotle pepper in adobo
- A pinch of salt and black pepper
- 5 colored bell peppers, tops and insides scooped out
- 1/2 cup vegan enchilada sauce
- 1 tablespoon chili powder
- 3 garlic cloves, minced
- 2 teaspoon cumin, ground

Directions:

1. Heat up a pan with the oil over medium high heat, add onion and celery, stir and cook for 5 minutes.
2. Add garlic, stir, cook for 1 minute more, take off heat and mix with chili, cumin and oregano.
3. Also add rice, corn, beans, tomato, salt, pepper and chipotle pepper and stir well.
4. Stuff bell peppers with this mix and place them in your slow cooker.
5. Add enchilada sauce, cover and cook on Low for 4 hours.
6. Arrange stuffed bell peppers on a platter and serve them as an appetizer. Enjoy!

Nutritional Value (Amount per Serving):

Calories: 221; Fat: 5g; Carb: 19g; Protein: 3g

Black Eyed Peas Pate

Prep Time: 10 Minutes
Cook Time: 5 Hours
Serves: 5

Ingredients:

- 1 and 1/2 cups black-eyed peas
- 3 cups water
- 1 teaspoon Cajun seasoning
- 1/2 cup pecans, toasted
- 1/2 teaspoon garlic powder
- 1/2 teaspoon jalapeno powder
- A pinch of salt and black pepper
- 1/4 teaspoon liquid smoke
- 1/2 teaspoon Tabasco sauce

Directions:

1. In your slow cooker, mix black-eyed pea with Cajun seasoning, salt, pepper and water, stir, cover and cook on High for 5 hours.
2. Drain, transfer to a blender, add pecans, garlic powder, jalapeno powder, Tabasco sauce, liquid smoke, more salt and pepper, pulse well and serve as an appetizer.

Enjoy!

Nutritional Value (Amount per Serving):

Calories: 221; Fat: 4g; Carb: 16g; Protein: 4g

Tofu Appetizer

Prep Time: 10 Minutes
Cook Time: 7 Hours
Serves: 6

Ingredients:

- 1/4 cup yellow onions, sliced
- 1 cup carrot, sliced
- 14 ounces firm tofu, cubed
- For the sauce:
- 1/4 cup soy sauce
- 1/2 cup water
- 3 tablespoons agave nectar
- 3 tablespoons nutritional yeast
- 1 tablespoon garlic, minced
- 1 tablespoon ginger, minced
- 1/2 tablespoon rice vinegar

Directions:

1. In your slow cooker, mix tofu with onion and carrots.
2. In a bowl, mix soy sauce with water, agave nectar, yeast, garlic, ginger and vinegar and whisk well.
3. Add this to slow cooker, cover and cook on Low for 7 hours.
4. Divide into appetizer bowls and serve.

Enjoy!

Nutritional Value (Amount per Serving):

Calories: 251; Fat: 6g; Carb: 12g; Protein: 3g

Artichoke Spread

Prep Time: 10 Minutes
Cook Time: 2 Hours
Serves: 8

Ingredients:

- 28 ounces canned artichokes, drained and chopped
- 10 ounces spinach
- 8 ounces coconut cream
- 1 yellow onion, chopped
- 2 garlic cloves, minced
- 3/4 cup coconut milk
- 1/2 cup tofu, pressed and crumbled
- 1/3 cup vegan avocado mayonnaise
- 1 tablespoon red vinegar
- A pinch of salt and black pepper

Directions:

1. In your slow cooker, mix artichokes with spinach, coconut cream, onion, garlic, coconut milk, tofu, avocado mayo, vinegar, salt and pepper, stir well, cover and cook on Low for 2 hours.
2. Divide into bowls and serve as an appetizer.
Enjoy!

Nutritional Value (Amount per Serving):

Calories: 355; Fat: 24g; Carb: 19g; Protein: 13g

Black Bean Appetizer Salad

Prep Time: 10 Minutes
Cook Time: 4 Hours
Serves: 7

Ingredients:

- 1 tablespoon coconut aminos
- 1/2 teaspoon cumin, ground
- 1 cup canned black beans
- 1 cup salsa
- 6 cups romaine lettuce leaves
- 1/2 cup avocado, peeled, pitted and mashed

Directions:

1. In your slow cooker, mix black beans with salsa, cumin and aminos, stir, cover and cook on Low for 4 hours.
2. In a salad bowl, mix lettuce leaves with black beans mix and mashed avocado, toss and serve as an appetizer.

Enjoy!

Nutritional Value (Amount per Serving):

Calories: 221; Fat: 4g; Carb: 12g; Protein: 3g

Three Bean Dip

Prep Time: 10 Minutes
Cook Time: 1 Hours
Serves: 6

Ingredients:

- 1/2 cup salsa
- 2 cups canned refried beans
- 1 cup vegan nacho cheese
- 2 tablespoons green onions, chopped

Directions:

1. In your slow cooker, mix refried beans with salsa, vegan nacho cheese and green onions, stir, cover and cook on High for 1 hour.
2. Divide into bowls and serve as a party snack.
Enjoy!

Nutritional Value (Amount per Serving):

Calories: 262; Fat: 5g; Carb: 20g; Protein: 3g

Great Bolognese Dip

Prep Time: 10 Minutes
Cook Time: 5 Hours
Serves: 7

Ingredients:

- 1/2 cauliflower head, riced in your blender
- 54 ounces canned tomatoes, crushed
- 10 ounces white mushrooms, chopped
- 2 cups carrots, shredded
- 2 cups eggplant, cubed
- 6 garlic cloves, minced
- 2 tablespoons agave nectar
- 2 tablespoons balsamic vinegar
- 2 tablespoons tomato paste
- 1 tablespoon basil, chopped
- 1 and 1/2 tablespoons oregano, chopped
- 1 and 1/2 teaspoons rosemary, dried
- A pinch of salt and black pepper

Directions:

1. In your slow cooker, mix cauliflower rice with tomatoes, mushrooms, carrots, eggplant cubes, garlic, agave nectar, balsamic vinegar, tomato paste, rosemary, salt and pepper, stir, cover and cook on High for 5 hours.
2. Add basil and oregano, stir again, divide into bowls and serve as a dip. Enjoy!

Nutritional Value (Amount per Serving):

Calories: 251; Fat: 7g; Carb: 10g; Protein: 6g

Eggplant Appetizer

Prep Time: 10 Minutes
Cook Time: 7 Hours
Serves: 4

Ingredients:

- 1 and 1/2 cups tomatoes, chopped
- 3 cups eggplant, cubed
- 2 teaspoons capers
- 6 ounces green olives, pitted and sliced
- 4 garlic cloves, minced
- 2 teaspoons balsamic vinegar
- 1 tablespoon basil, chopped
- Salt and black pepper to the taste

Directions:

1. In your slow cooker, mix tomatoes with eggplant cubes, capers, green olives, garlic, vinegar, basil, salt and pepper, toss, cover and cook on Low for 7 hours.
2. Divide into small appetizer plates and serve as an appetizer.
Enjoy!

Nutritional Value (Amount per Serving):

Calories: 200; Fat: 6g; Carb: 9g; Protein: 2g

Chapter 7: Beef, Pork & Lamb

Savory Smoky Pulled Pork

Prep Time: 10 Minutes

Cook Time: 9 Hours

Serves: 6

Ingredients:

- 1 (2-pound) pork shoulder (also known as Boston butt), trimmed of excess fat
- ½ cup chicken broth
- 1 tablespoon tamari or low-sodium soy sauce
- 1 tablespoon liquid smoke
- 1 garlic clove, minced

Directions:

1. Cut the pork roast into four equal pieces and put them in the slow cooker. Put the broth, liquid smoke, soy sauce, and garlic over the pork.
2. Cover with the lid and cook on low for 9 hours.
3. Remove the pork to a carving board and shred the meat. Serve bon appetite.

Nutritional Value (Amount per Serving):

Calories: 392; Fat: 31g; Carb: 0g; Protein: 26g

Special St. Louis—Style Ribs

Prep Time: 10 Minutes
Cook Time: 8 Hours
Serves: 4

Ingredients:

- 1 (2½-pound) rack St. Louis–style pork ribs
- 2½ teaspoons barbecue seasoning
- 1 cup water
- ½ cup barbecue sauce

Directions:

1. Rub the rack of ribs with the barbecue seasoning and place it in the slow cooker. Coil the ribs around the walls of the slow cooker with the meaty side facing out. Move the water into the slow cooker.
2. Cover with the lid and cook on low for 8 hours.
3. Spoon the barbecue sauce on the top of the ribs and serve immediately.

Nutritional Value (Amount per Serving):

Calories: 547; Fat: 33g; Carb: 11g; Protein: 50g

Authentic Mexican Pulled Pork

Prep Time: 10 Minutes
Cook Time: 9 Hours
Serves: 6

Ingredients:

- 1 large yellow onion, cut into thick slices
- 1 cup chicken broth
- 1 (2-pound) pork shoulder (also known as Boston butt), trimmed of excess fat
- 1 (14.5-ounce) can diced tomatoes with jalapeños
- 1 tablespoon tomato paste
- ¾ teaspoon garlic salt
- ½ teaspoon dried oregano
- Salt
- Freshly ground black pepper

Directions:

1. Place the onion slices in the slow cooker. Put in the broth. Move the pork on top of the onions.
2. Cover with the lid and cook on low for 9 hours, or until the meat is very soft.
3. Remove the pork to a cutting board and shred the meat with two forks. Discard the onions and liquid in the slow cooker. Move the meat back to the slow cooker.
4. Switch the slow cooker to high. Add the tomatoes with their juice, garlic salt, tomato paste, and oregano. Stir the meat until equally coated. Cover and cook for a few minutes, until heated completely. Season with salt and pepper and serve bon appetite.

Nutritional Value (Amount per Serving):

Calories: 417; Fat: 31g; Carb: 6g; Protein: 27g

Savory Pork and Broccoli

Prep Time: 10 Minutes
Cook Time: 8 Hours
Serves: 6

Ingredients:

- 1 cup beef broth
- ¼ cup tamari or low-sodium soy sauce
- ¼ cup oyster sauce
- 1 teaspoon toasted sesame oil
- ¼ cup (packed) brown sugar
- 1 teaspoon garlic powder
- 2 pounds pork stew meat
- ¼ cup cornstarch
- ¼ cup water
- 1 (16-ounce) package frozen broccoli

Directions:

1. Combine the tamari, beef broth, sesame oil, brown sugar, oyster sauce, and garlic powder in the slow cooker. Blend until smooth. Add the pork and stir to coat with the sauce.
2. Cover with the lid and cook on low for 8 hours.
3. Remove the lid and turn to high. Make a slurry by stirring together the cornstarch and water in a small bowl. Put the slurry to the slow cooker and stir fully; the liquid should thicken a bit.
4. Place the frozen broccoli in a colander and run hot water over it until it's heated through. Shake off the excess liquid. Blend the broccoli into the slow cooker. Let the sauce thicken for about 10 minutes before serving.

Nutritional Value (Amount per Serving):

Calories: 319; Fat: 12g; Carb: 17g; Protein: 34g

Savory Cilantro-Lime Shredded Pork

Prep Time: 5 Minutes
Cook Time: 8 Hours
Serves: 6 To 8

Ingredients:

- 2½ pounds country-style pork ribs, trimmed of excess fat
- ¼ cup fresh lime juice
- 1 tablespoon chili powder
- 1 tablespoon ground cumin
- 2 teaspoons salt
- ½ cup chopped fresh cilantro

Directions:

1. Place the pork in the slow cooker. Pour the lime juice over the pork and spritz with the cumin, chili powder, and salt.
2. Cover with the lid and cook on low for 8 hours.
3. Remove the pork to a cutting board and shred the meat with two forks. Return the pork to the slow cooker and whisk. Add the chopped cilantro and serve bon appetite.

Nutritional Value (Amount per Serving):

Calories: 360; Fat: 22g; Carb: 2g; Protein: 37g

Tasty Smothered Pork Chops

Prep Time: 10 Minutes
Cook Time: 4 Hours
Serves: 4

Ingredients:

- ½ cup finely diced onion
- 5 slices cooked bacon, crumbled, divided
- ½ cup chicken broth
- 2 teaspoons tamari or low-sodium soy sauce
- ¼ cup flour
- 1 teaspoon garlic powder
- ½ teaspoon dried thyme
- ½ teaspoon brown sugar
- Freshly ground black pepper
- 1½ teaspoons apple cider vinegar
- 1 bay leaf
- 4 bone-in pork chops
- Salt

Directions:

1. Place the onion and half of the bacon crumbles in the slow cooker. Whisk together the broth, tamari, flour, garlic powder, thyme, and brown sugar in a small bowl. Pour the mixture into the slow cooker. Add the bay leaf.
2. Nestle the pork chops in the slow cooker. Gently season the chops with pepper and salt.
3. Cover with the lid and cook on low for 4 hours.
4. Remove the pork chops to a serving platter and tent loosely with aluminum foil to keep warm. Let them rest for about 10 minutes.
5. Discard the bay leaf. Blend the vinegar into the sauce in the slow cooker. Spoon the sauce over the pork chops. Top with the rest of the bacon crumbles and serve.

Nutritional Value (Amount per Serving):

Calories: 516; Fat: 34g; Carb: 11g; Protein: 46g

Delicious Cajun Pork Steaks

Prep Time: 10 Minutes
Cook Time: 8 Hours
Serves: 4

Ingredients:

- 1½ pounds pork shoulder steaks, trimmed of excess fat
- Salt
- Freshly ground black pepper
- 1 cup barbecue sauce
- 1 teaspoon Cajun seasoning
- ½ teaspoon garlic powder
- ½ teaspoon onion powder

Directions:

1. Place the pork steaks in the slow cooker. Gently season with salt and pepper.
2. Stir together the barbecue sauce, Cajun seasoning, garlic powder, and onion powder in a small bowl. Pour the mixture over the pork.
3. Cover and cook on low for 8 hours. Serve bon appetite.

Nutritional Value (Amount per Serving):

Calories: 486; Fat: 32g; Carb: 23g; Protein: 25g

Special Hoisin Pork Sliders

Prep Time: 5 Minutes
Cook Time: 9 Hours
Serves: 6

Ingredients:

- 1 (2-pound) picnic pork roast, trimmed of excess fat
- 1 cup chicken broth
- 3 tablespoons hoisin sauce
- 2 tablespoons tamari or low-sodium soy sauce
- 1 teaspoon minced fresh ginger
- 1 teaspoon garlic powder
- Hawaiian sweet rolls, for serving

Directions:

1. Cut the pork roast into four equal pieces. Place the pork in the slow cooker. Put the broth over the pork.
2. Cover with the lid and cook on low for around 9 hours, or until the pork is fork-tender.
3. Remove the pork to a cutting board and shred with two forks. Discard the broth in the slow cooker and move the pork back to the slow cooker.
4. Whisk together the hoisin sauce, tamari, ginger, and garlic powder in a small bowl. Pour the sauce into the slow cooker and whisk to coat the pork.
5. Cover with the lid and cook on high for 10 more minutes. Serve the shredded pork on Hawaiian sweet rolls.

Nutritional Value (Amount per Serving):

Calories: 417; Fat: 32g; Carb: 5g; Protein: 27g

Delicious Country-Style Ribs

Prep Time: 10 Minutes
Cook Time: 8 Hours
Serves: 6

Ingredients:

- 2 pounds boneless country-style pork ribs, trimmed of excess fat
- ¼ cup apple cider vinegar
- ¼ cup ketchup
- 1½ tablespoons brown sugar
- 1½ teaspoon chili powder
- ½ teaspoon smoked paprika
- ½ teaspoon ground cumin
- ½ teaspoon salt
- ¼ teaspoon freshly ground black pepper

Directions:

1. Place the ribs in the slow cooker.
2. Whisk together the vinegar, ketchup, brown sugar, chili powder, paprika, cumin, salt, and pepper in a small bowl. Pour the sauce over the ribs.
3. Cover with the lid and cook on low for 8 hours. Serve the ribs together with the pan juices.

Nutritional Value (Amount per Serving):

Calories: 394; Fat: 29g; Carb: 8g; Protein: 26g

Simple Buffalo Pork Lettuce Wraps

Prep Time: 5 Minutes
Cook Time: 8 Hours
Serves: 6

Ingredients:

- 1 (2-pound) picnic pork roast, trimmed of excess fat
- 1 small yellow onion, quartered
- 1 cup chicken broth
- ½ cup buffalo sauce
- 6 large romaine lettuce leaves

Directions:

1. Place the pork roast in the slow cooker. Nestle the onion quarters around the pork. Place the broth over the pork.
2. Cover with the lid and cook on low for 8 hours.
3. Remove the pork to a cutting board. Shred the pork with two forks. Discard the liquid and onion in the slow cooker. Remove the meat to the slow cooker, pour in the buffalo sauce, and stir to mix. Put a heaping portion of pork on each romaine leaf and roll it up, and then eat.

Nutritional Value (Amount per Serving):

Calories: 400; Fat: 31g; Carb: 2g; Protein: 26g

Delicious Meat Sauce

Prep Time: 10 Minutes
Cook Time: 8 Hours
Serves: 8

Ingredients:

- 8 ounces lean ground beef
- 1 pound ground Italian pork sausage
- 1 (28-ounce) can crushed tomatoes
- 1 (14.5-ounce) can diced tomatoes with green peppers, celery, and onions
- 2 tablespoons tomato paste
- 1 bay leaf
- 2 teaspoons dried basil
- 1 teaspoon garlic powder
- 1 teaspoon brown sugar
- ½ teaspoon dried oregano
- Salt
- Freshly ground black pepper

Directions:

1. Mix the ground beef and ground Italian sausage in the slow cooker. Break up the meat with the help of a wooden spoon. Add the diced tomatoes, crushed tomatoes with their juice, tomato paste, garlic powder, brown sugar, bay leaf, basil, and oregano. Stir well to combine.
2. Cover with the lid and cook on low for 8 hours.
3. Discard the bay leaf and whisk. Season with pepper and salt and serve.

Nutritional Value (Amount per Serving):

Calories: 295; Fat: 18g; Carb: 13g; Protein: 20g

Juicy Lamb Steaks

Prep Time: 10 Minutes
Cook Time: 5 Hours
Serves: 4

Ingredients:

- 3 garlic cloves, minced
- ¼ teaspoon salt, plus more for seasoning
- ¼ teaspoon freshly ground black pepper, plus more for seasoning
- 4 (4-ounce) boneless top round lamb steaks, trimmed of excess fat
- ½ cup chicken broth
- 1 tablespoon chopped fresh basil
- 1 tablespoon chopped fresh mint
- ¼ cup chopped grape tomatoes

Directions:

1. Stir together the minced garlic, salt, and pepper in a small bowl. Rub the lamb steaks with the garlic mixture and move them in the slow cooker. Pour in the broth.
2. Cover with the lid and cook on low for 5 hours.
3. Remove the lamb steaks to a serving platter. Season with more salt and pepper. Top the lamb with a sprinkling of mint, basil, and tomatoes and serve bon appetite.

Nutritional Value (Amount per Serving):

Calories: 301; Fat: 24g; Carb: 3g; Protein: 19g

Savory Lamb Gyros

Prep Time: 5 Minutes
Cook Time: 8 Hours
Serves: 6

Ingredients:

- 2 pounds lamb shoulder or leg chops
- ¼ cup fresh lemon juice
- 1 teaspoon garlic powder
- 1 teaspoon dried oregano
- 1 teaspoon salt
- ½ teaspoon freshly ground black pepper
- Pita bread, for serving
- Chopped red onion, for serving
- Tzatziki sauce, for serving

Directions:

1. Place the lamb in the slow cooker.
2. Whisk together the lemon juice, garlic powder, oregano, salt, and pepper in a small bowl. Pour the mixture over the lamb.
3. Cover with the lid and cook on low for 8 hours.
4. Remove the meat to a cutting board. Slices the meat into bite-size pieces and put on a platter. Serve each gyro with the lamb wrapped in pita and topped with tzatziki sauce and chopped onion. Serve

Nutritional Value (Amount per Serving):

Calories: 441; Fat: 19g; Carb: 20g; Protein: 47g

Chapter 8: Soup

Savory Beef and Barley Soup

Prep Time: 15 Minutes
Cook Time: 8 Hours
Serves: 6 To 8

Ingredients:

- 3 cups chicken broth
- 3 cups beef broth
- 1 tablespoon tomato paste
- 2 cups frozen mirepoix
- 1½ pounds beef chuck roast, trimmed of excess fat and cut into bite-size pieces
- ⅔ cup pearl barley (not quick-cooking)
- 8 ounces sliced mushrooms
- 1 bay leaf
- 1 teaspoon onion powder
- 1 teaspoon garlic powder
- ¾ teaspoon dried thyme
- 1 teaspoon salt, plus more for seasoning
- ½ teaspoon freshly ground black pepper, plus more for seasoning

Directions:

1. Combine all the ingredients in the slow cooker and mix.
2. Cover with the lid and cook on low for 8 hours.
3. Discard the bay leaf. Season with additional pepper and salt, if necessary. Ladle into bowls and serve bon appetite.

Nutritional Value (Amount per Serving):

Calories: 298; Fat: 9g; Carb: 21g; Protein: 31g

Delicious Tomato Soup

Prep Time: 10 Minutes
Cook Time: 8 Hours
Serves: 6

Ingredients:

- 1 cup frozen mirepoix
- ⅓ cup all-purpose flour
- 1 (28-ounce) can crushed tomatoes
- 1 (6-ounce) can tomato paste
- 1 tablespoon dried basil
- 1 teaspoon dried oregano
- 1 teaspoon salt, plus more for seasoning
- 4 cups chicken or vegetable broth
- 1 bay leaf
- 1 cup milk, warmed
- 2 tablespoons unsalted butter
- Freshly ground black pepper
- ⅔ cup grated Parmesan cheese

Directions:

1. Mix the flour, mirepoix, tomato paste, crushed tomatoes, basil, oregano, and salt in the slow cooker. Use a whisk to blend the flour into the tomatoes to incorporate. Add the broth and blend. Add the bay leaf.
2. Cover with the lid and cook on low for 8 hours.
3. Discard the bay leaf. Stir in the butter and warm milk until the butter is melted. Season with additional salt and pepper, if you like.
4. Ladle the soup into bowls, put Parmesan cheese on the top, and serve.

Nutritional Value (Amount per Serving):

Calories: 200; Fat: 8g; Carb: 25g; Protein: 11g

Savory Black Bean Soup

Prep Time: 10 Minutes
Cook Time: 8 Hours
Serves: 6

Ingredients:

- 8 ounces dried black beans, picked over and rinsed
- 3½ cups water
- 1 smoked ham hock, rinsed
- 1 bay leaf
- 1 teaspoon dried oregano
- 1 teaspoon ground cumin
- 1 teaspoon garlic powder
- 1 teaspoon salt, plus more for seasoning
- Juice of 1 lime
- 1 (8-ounce) can tomato sauce
- Freshly ground black pepper
- Chopped fresh cilantro, for garnish

Directions:

1. Combine the bay leaf, water, ham hock, black beans, cumin, oregano, garlic powder, and salt in the slow cooker.
2. Cover with the lid and cook on low for 8 hours, or until the beans are soft.
3. Discard the bay leaf. Blend in the lime juice and tomato sauce. Season with additional salt and pepper, if you like.
4. Ladle into soup bowls and garnish with cilantro, serve bon appetite.

Nutritional Value (Amount per Serving):

Calories: 237; Fat: 7g; Carb: 23g; Protein: 21g

Delicious French Onion Soup

Prep Time: 15 Minutes
Cook Time: 8 Hours
Serves: 4

Ingredients:

- 3 small yellow onions, cut into thin rings
- ¼ cup olive oil or canola oil
- Pinch salt
- Pinch freshly ground black pepper
- Pinch sugar
- 2 (13.5-ounce) cans beef consommé
- ½ cup water
- 4 slices crusty bread (French bread or a baguette works well)
- 1⅓ cups shredded Gruyère cheese

Directions:

1. Place the onions in the slow cooker. Add the salt, pepper, olive oil, and sugar and stir until the onions are well coated.
2. Cover with the lid and cook on low for 8 hours, or until the onions are tender and caramelized.
3. Put in the consommé and water and turn the slow cooker to high. Cook until heated through, about 10 minutes.
4. Position the top oven rack about 6 inches below the broiler. Switch on the broiler.
5. Ladle the soup into four oven-safe bowls and put them on a rimmed baking sheet. Put a piece of bread on the top of each serving of soup. Spray ⅓ cup of Gruyère cheese on the top of each piece of bread.
6. Broil for about 1 to 2 minutes, or until the cheese is melted and starts to brown. Serve right away.

Nutritional Value (Amount per Serving):

Calories: 384; Fat: 24g; Carb: 28g; Protein: 17g

Savory Lemony Lentil and Chicken Soup

Prep Time: 15 Minutes
Cook Time: 6 Hours
Serves: 6

Ingredients:

- 1 medium yellow onion, very thinly sliced
- 1 cup brown lentils
- 1 pound boneless, skinless chicken thighs, trimmed of excess fat
- 1 teaspoon garlic powder
- 5 cups chicken broth
- 3 large egg yolks
- ¼ cup fresh lemon juice
- Salt
- Freshly ground black pepper

Directions:

1. Combine the chicken, garlic powder, onion, lentils, and chicken broth in the slow cooker.
2. Cover with the lid and cook on low for 6 hours.
3. Remove the chicken to a cutting board. Shred the chicken with two forks and move it back to the slow cooker.
4. Whisk together the egg yolks and lemon juice in a small bowl. Stir the mixture into the slow cooker. Season with salt and pepper and serve bon appetite.

Nutritional Value (Amount per Serving):

Calories: 277; Fat: 8g; Carb: 23g; Protein: 29g

Savory Mexican Corn Chowder

Prep Time: 15 Minutes
Cook Time: 8 Hours
Serves: 6 To 8

Ingredients:

- 1 (16-ounce) package frozen sweet white corn kernels
- 1 teaspoon salt, plus more for seasoning
- ½ teaspoon freshly ground black pepper, plus more for seasoning
- ½ teaspoon ground cumin
- 4 cups chicken broth
- ½ cup picante sauce
- 4 medium russet potatoes, peeled (about 1½ pounds total)
- 4 bone-in, skinless chicken thighs, trimmed of excess fat
- 2 to 3 tablespoons fresh lime juice

Directions:

1. Put the corn in the slow cooker. Spray in the pepper, salt, and cumin. Pour in the broth and the picante sauce. Submerge the potatoes in the liquid. Nestle the chicken thighs in among the potatoes.
2. Cover with the lid and cook on low for 8 hours.
3. Remove the chicken to a cutting board. The meat should practically fall off the bones. Discard the cartilage and bones. Shred the chicken with two forks and move it back to the slow cooker.
4. Remove the potatoes to the cutting board. Smash two of the potatoes with a fork and blend into the slow cooker. Cut the remaining two potatoes into cubes. Softly mix the cubed potatoes and lime juice into the slow cooker. Season with additional salt and pepper, if necessary. Ladle the soup into bowls and serve bon appetite.

Nutritional Value (Amount per Serving):

Calories: 250; Fat: 4g; Carb: 31g; Protein: 22g

Delicious Broccoli Cheddar Soup

Prep Time: 10 Minutes
Cook Time: 8 Hours
Serves: 5

Ingredients:

- 2 cups chicken broth
- 1 pound Yukon Gold potatoes, peeled
- 1 medium yellow onion, diced
- 2 scallions, minced
- ¼ teaspoon ground thyme
- 1 teaspoon garlic powder
- Salt
- Freshly ground black pepper
- 1 (1-pound) package frozen broccoli florets, thawed and drained
- ½ cup shredded extra-sharp Cheddar cheese
- ½ cup milk
- 1 tablespoon unsalted butter

Directions:

1. Combine the onion, scallions, garlic powder, broth, potatoes, and thyme in the slow cooker. Season with pepper and salt.
2. Cover with the lid and cook on low for 8 hours.
3. Carefully remove the contents of the slow cooker to a blender, in batches if desired. Purée until smooth, making sure to vent the blender lid for steam. Add three-quarters of the broccoli. Pulse three or four times to get the soup to your favorite consistency.
4. Move the soup back into the slow cooker. Add the butter, Cheddar, milk, and remaining broccoli and mix. Season with additional salt and pepper, if necessary.
5. Switch the slow cooker to high and cook for a few minutes, until warmed through. Serve bon appetite.

Nutritional Value (Amount per Serving):

Calories: 194; Fat: 8g; Carb: 24g; Protein: 10g

Savory Chicken Enchilada Soup

Prep Time: 10 Minutes
Cook Time: 8 Hours
Serves: 6

Ingredients:

- 1 cup chicken broth
- 1½ cups picante sauce
- 1 (15-ounce) can enchilada sauce
- 1 (14.5-ounce) can black beans, rinsed and drained
- 1½ pounds boneless, skinless chicken thighs, trimmed of excess fat
- 1 teaspoon ground cumin
- 1 (14.5-ounce) can refried beans
- Sour cream, for topping (optional)

Directions:

1. Combine the enchilada sauce, black beans, chicken, broth, picante sauce, and cumin in the slow cooker.
2. Cover with the lid and cook on low for 8 hours.
3. Remove the chicken to a cutting board. It should be very soft. Shred the chicken with two forks.
4. Put the refried beans to the slow cooker and mix until combined. Softly stir in the shredded chicken. Ladle the soup into bowls, top each serving with a dollop of sour cream (if you like), and serve bon appetite.

Nutritional Value (Amount per Serving):

Calories: 273; Fat: 8g; Carb: 22g; Protein: 28g

Tasty Chicken and Pesto Soup

Prep Time: 15 Minutes
Cook Time: 6 Hours
Serves: 6

Ingredients:

- 3½ cups chicken broth
- 2 carrots, peeled and cut into ¼-inch rounds
- 2 celery stalks, cut into ¼-inch slices
- 1 teaspoon dried oregano
- 1 teaspoon garlic powder
- 5 boneless, skinless chicken thighs, trimmed of excess fat
- ½ cup long-grain brown rice
- 1½ cups milk, at room temperature
- ½ cup basil pesto

Directions:

1. Combine the celery, oregano, broth, carrots, and garlic powder in the slow cooker and mix. Add the chicken and rice and mix.
2. Cover with the lid and cook on low for 6 hours, or until the chicken is cooked through and the rice is soft.
3. Remove the chicken to a cutting board. Shred the chicken with two forks or cut it into small pieces. Move the chicken back to the slow cooker. Stir in the milk and pesto.
4. Cover with the lid and cook on high for 10 minutes, until warmed through. Ladle into bowls and serve bon appetite.

Nutritional Value (Amount per Serving):

Calories: 239; Fat: 8g; Carb: 18g; Protein: 25g

Flavory Chicken and Barley Soup

Prep Time: 10 Minutes
Cook Time: 6 Hours
Serves: 6

Ingredients:

- 5 boneless, skinless chicken thighs, trimmed of excess fat
- ½ cup pearl barley (not quick-cooking)
- 3 cups frozen mirepoix
- 3½ cups chicken broth
- 1 (14.5-ounce) can diced tomatoes, undrained
- 1 tablespoon tomato paste
- 1 bay leaf
- 1 teaspoon dried basil
- 1 teaspoon garlic powder
- ¾ teaspoon salt, plus more for seasoning
- ¼ teaspoon freshly ground black pepper, plus more for seasoning

Directions:

1. Mix all the ingredients in the slow cooker and blend to combine.
2. Cover with the lid and cook on low for 6 hours.
3. Discard the bay leaf. Remove the chicken to a cutting board. Shred the chicken with two forks or cut it into small pieces. Move the chicken back to the slow cooker. Season with additional pepper and salt, if you like. Ladle the soup into bowls and serve bon appetite.

Nutritional Value (Amount per Serving):

Calories: 164; Fat: 6g; Carb: 6g; Protein: 22g

Delicious Creamy Cauliflower-Broccoli Soup

Prep Time: 10 Minutes
Cook Time: 8 Hours
Serves: 6

Ingredients:

- 2 pounds cauliflower florets
- 2 scallions, minced
- 2 cups chicken or vegetable broth
- 1 teaspoon onion powder
- 1 teaspoon garlic powder
- ¼ teaspoon dried thyme
- ½ teaspoon salt, plus more for seasoning
- ¼ teaspoon freshly ground black pepper, plus more for seasoning
- 1 (12-ounce) package frozen broccoli florets
- ½ cup grated Parmesan cheese, plus more for optional garnish
- ¼ cup heavy cream

Directions:

1. Combine the broth, onion powder, thyme, salt, cauliflower, scallions, garlic powder, and pepper in the slow cooker.
2. Cover with the lid and cook on low for 8 hours.
3. Carefully remove the contents of the slow cooker to a blender, in batches if needed. Purée until smooth, making sure to vent the blender lid for steam. Pour the puréed soup back into the slow cooker.
4. Blend in the Parmesan cheese, broccoli, and cream. Cover with the lid and cook on high for 10 minutes, or until heated through.
5. Season with additional pepper and salt, if necessary. Ladle the soup into bowls and garnish with more Parmesan cheese, if you like.

Nutritional Value (Amount per Serving):

Calories: 124; Fat: 5g; Carb: 14g; Protein: 10g

Flavor-packed Ham and White Bean Soup

Prep Time: 10 Minutes (Plus Soaking The Beans Overnight)
Cook Time: 8 Hours
Serves: 8

Ingredients:

- 1 pound dried great northern beans, picked over and rinsed
- 1 tablespoon salt, plus ½ teaspoon, divided
- 6 cups chicken broth
- 6 cups water
- 2 cups cubed ham
- 2 cups frozen mirepoix
- 1 teaspoon dried basil
- 1 teaspoon dried oregano
- ¼ teaspoon freshly ground black pepper, plus more for seasoning
- 2 bay leaves
- ½ teaspoon liquid smoke

Directions:

1. The night before you make the soup, place the beans in a large bowl and add enough water to cover them by 2 inches. Spray in 1 tablespoon of salt. Soak the beans for more than 8 hours.
2. The next day, drain the water and rinse the beans completly. Place the beans in the slow cooker. Add the chicken broth, 6 cups fresh water, basil, oregano, ham, mirepoix, remaining ½ teaspoon of salt, pepper, bay leaves, water, and liquid smoke.
3. Cover with the lid and cook on low for 8 hours, or until the beans are soft.
4. Discard the bay leaves. Season with additional pepper and salt, if you like. Ladle into bowls and serve bon appetite.

Nutritional Value (Amount per Serving):

Calories: 287; Fat: 3g; Carb: 42g; Protein: 24g

Chapter 9: Rice & Beans

Chicken on Rice with Cheese

Prep Time: 10 Minutes
Cook Time: 6 Hours
Serves: 8

Ingredients:

- 1 ½ lbs chicken breasts, boneless & diced
- 2 cups long-grain rice, uncooked
- 2 cups cheddar cheese, grated
- 12 oz frozen peas & carrots
- 3 cups chicken broth
- 1 can cream of chicken soup

Directions:

1. Place chicken breasts and remaining ingredients into the slow cooker and mix them well.
2. Cover lid on, and cook on low- temperature mode for 6 hours.
3. Serve warm.

Nutritional Value (Amount per Serving):

Calories: 513; Fat: 18.9g; Carb: 44.7g; Protein: 39g

Flavored Mushroom Rice

Prep Time: 10 Minutes

Cook Time: 2 Hours

Serves: 8

Ingredients:

- 2 cups rice
- 1 lb mushrooms, sliced & sautéed
- 4 cups beef broth
- ½ tsp thyme, dried
- 2 garlic cloves, minced
- 1 onion, diced & sautéed
- 3 tbsp butter, melted
- Pepper
- Salt

Directions:

1. Add melted butter, rice, and remaining ingredients into the slow cooker and mix them well.
2. Cover lid on, and cook on high- temperature mode for 2 hours.
3. Serve warm.

Nutritional Value (Amount per Serving):

Calories: 245; Fat: 5.5g; Carb: 40.9g; Protein: 7.8g

Spanish- flavored Rice

Prep Time: 10 Minutes
Cook Time: 3 Hours
Serves: 12

Ingredients:

- 2 cups rice, uncooked
- 2 tbsp cilantro, chopped
- 1 ½ tsp cumin, ground
- 2 tsp chili powder
- 2 bell peppers, diced
- 1 ½ tsp garlic, minced
- 14 oz can tomatoes, diced
- 2 cups tomato sauce
- 2 cups chicken stock
- 1 onion, diced
- 2 tbsp olive oil
- 1 ½ tsp salt

Directions:

1. Add rice and remaining ingredients into the slow cooker and mix them well.
2. Cover lid on, and cook on high- temperature mode for 3 hours.
3. Serve warm.e.

Nutritional Value (Amount per Serving):

Calories: 169; Fat: 3g; Carb: 31.5g; Protein: 4.3g

Healthy Herbed Brown Rice

Prep Time: 10 Minutes
Cook Time: 3 Hours
Serves: 4

Ingredients:

- 2 cups brown rice
- ½ tsp oregano. dried
- ½ tsp thyme, dried
- 4 cups chicken stock
- 8 oz mushrooms, sliced
- 2 tbsp butter, melted
- Pepper
- Salt

Directions:

1. Add brown rice, oregano, thyme, broth, mushrooms, butter, pepper, and salt into the slow cooker and mix them well.
2. Cover lid on, and cook on high- temperature mode for 3 hours.
3. Serve warm.

Nutritional Value (Amount per Serving):

Calories: 446; Fat: 9.9g; Carb: 75.4g; Protein: 13.9g

Pinto bacon Beans with Tomato

Prep Time: 10 Minutes
Cook Time: 8 Hours
Serves: 6

Ingredients:

- 1 lb pinto beans, soaked overnight & drained
- 15 oz can tomatoes, diced
- 8 bacon slices, cooked & crumbled
- 14 oz beef broth
- 32 oz vegetable broth
- 2 jalapenos, chopped
- 1 tsp cumin
- 1 tsp garlic powder
- 1 tbsp garlic, minced
- 1 medium onion, sliced
- Pepper
- Salt

Directions:

1. Add processed beans and remaining ingredients into the slow cooker and stir everything well.
2. Cover lid on, and cook on high- temperature mode for 8 hours.
3. Serve warm.

Nutritional Value (Amount per Serving):

Calories: 463; Fat: 12.9g; Carb: 55g; Protein: 31.1g

CONCLUSION

With all the things that keep you busy every day, it's definitely a good idea to invest in a slow cooker and use this to make healthy and flavorful dishes for you and your family without the stress.

Not only that, this also helps you save money in the long run as it uses less energy than other electric cooking devices.

Once you've gotten into the habit of slow cooking, you'll surely find yourself doing this often.

Enjoy slow cooking!

APPENDIX RECIPE INDEX